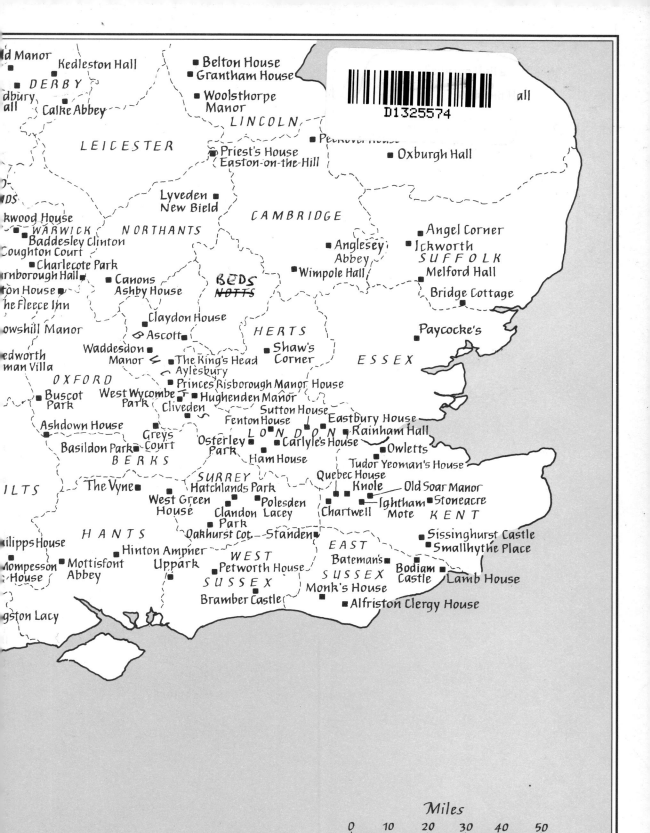

d Manor
Kedleston Hall
DERBY
dbury
all
Calke Abbey

Belton House
Grantham House
Woolsthorpe Manor
LINCOLN

LEICESTER

Peluoverhouse
Oxburgh Hall
Priest's House
Easton-on-the-Hill

Lyveden New Bield
CAMBRIDGE

Angel Corner
Ickworth
SUFFOLK
Melford Hall
Bridge Cottage

kwood House
WARWICK
Baddesley Clinton
Coughton Court
Charlecote Park
rnborough Hall
ton House
he Fleece Inn
owshill Manor
edworth
man Villa

NORTHANTS
Canons Ashby House

BEDS
~~NOTTS~~

Anglesey Abbey
Wimpole Hall

Paycocke's

Claydon House
Ascott
Waddesdon Manor
The King's Head Aylesbury
Princes Risborough Manor House

HERTS
Shaw's Corner

ESSEX

OXFORD
Buscot Park
Ashdown House
Greys Court
Basildon Park
BERKS

West Wycombe Park
Cliveden
Hughenden Manor
Sutton House
Fenton House
LONDON
Osterley Park
Carlyle's House
Ham House

Eastbury House
Rainham Hall
Owletts
Tudor Yeoman's House
Quebec House
Knole
Old Soar Manor

ILTS
The Vyne
West Green House
Hatchlands Park
SURREY
Polesden Lacey
Clandon Park
Oakhurst Cot.
Standen

Ightham Mote
Stoneacre
Chartwell
KENT

HANTS

ilipps House
Mompesson House
Mottisfont Abbey
Hinton Ampner
Uppark

WEST SUSSEX
Petworth House
SUSSEX
Bramber Castle

Bateman's
Monk's House
EAST SUSSEX

Bodiam Castle
Lamb House

Sissinghurst Castle
Smallhythe Place

gston Lacy

Alfriston Clergy House

Miles

0   10   20   30   40   50

HISTORIC HOUSES
OF THE
NATIONAL TRUST

HISTORIC HOUSES
— OF THE —
NATIONAL TRUST

Adrian Tinniswood

FOREWORD BY
Gervase Jackson-Stops

THE NATIONAL TRUST

For Helen

First published in Great Britain in 1991 by
National Trust Enterprises Limited
36 Queen Anne's Gate
London SW1H 9AS

British Library Cataloguing in Publication Data

Tinniswood, Adrian, 1954–
Historic houses of the National Trust.
I. Title II. National Trust
914.104859

ISBN 0-7078-0140-0

Picture research by Samantha Wyndham

Designed by Newton Engert Partnership

Maps drawn by N. S. Hyslop

Production by Bob Towell

Phototypeset in Monotype Lasercomp Baskerville 169
by Southern Positives and Negatives (SPAN), Lingfield, Surrey

Origination by Columbia Offset, Singapore

Manufactured in Italy by Grafedit S.p.A., Bergamo

HALF-TITLE:
Detail of one of William Burges's carved capitals at
Knightshayes Court, Devon. (*NTPL/John Bethell*)

FRONTISPIECE:
The staircase at Castle Drogo in Devon. (*NTPL*)

PAGE SEVEN:
The Duke of Somerset's arms and supporters – the bull
and the unicorn – over the chimneypiece in the marble hall
at Petworth, West Sussex. (*NTPL/James Pipkin*)

CONTENTS

CONTENTS

ACKNOWLEDGEMENTS

Many people have helped in the writing of this book. Margaret Willes, the Trust's Publisher, initiated the project, and she and Gervase Jackson-Stops were kind enough to read the whole manuscript, correcting numerous mistakes and making unfailingly helpful suggestions. Needless to say, the errors which remain are all my own work.

A number of colleagues and friends have also commented on individual parts of the text and given me the benefit of their specialised knowledge. I would particularly like to thank Martin Drury, Historic Buildings Secretary of the National Trust and all his regional representatives: James Lees-Milne, for sharing his memories of the early years of the Country Houses Scheme; David Thackray, the Trust's Chief Archaeological Adviser; Cherry Ann Knott for her considerable help with the section on Sudbury Hall; and John Hodgson for his good ideas. Thanks also to Caroline Henley for keeping her head when all around were losing theirs.

I am grateful to Samantha Wyndham for her diligent and inspired research on the pictures for the book. A large proportion of these come from the National Trust's Photo Library at Queen Anne's Gate, and are marked NTPL together with the name of the photographer. Those credited to the National Trust are either from regional photo libraries or from the Trust's historic archives.

Lastly, I would like to pay tribute to all those past and present staff members of the National Trust without whose research this book could not have been written, and without whose care and foresight many of the the houses described in it might not be here at all.

Adrian Tinniswood
April 1991

The long gallery at Sudbury Hall, Derbyshire. This was restored by the National Trust in 1969–70, with advice from John Fowler. (*The National Trust/John Roberts*)

Foreword

The public perception of the National Trust is now so bound up with the great houses in its ownership that few people realise how little they counted to its original founders. In fact the Trust has only seriously been concerned with country houses and their collections for a mere forty out of almost a hundred years of existence. And, even then, they seemed to come more by accident than design: as a way of avoiding the disastrous effects of capital taxation, rather than part of a deliberate policy of preservation.

However unplanned this development – in the manner of so many other British institutions – it has gathered its own momentum, and it is fascinating to look back on the shifts of emphasis that have occurred in that time, the very different reasons for acquiring houses then and now, and the changing priorities which the Trust faces in conserving and maintaining them.

Before the start of the Country Houses Scheme, described in the first chapter of this book, a few buildings were taken on by the Trust, usually to save them from imminent destruction, and usually because of their picturesque 'Old English' qualities. None of them dated from after 1600, and none of them contained significant contents, or even particularly significant interiors. Whether modest domestic dwellings like the Clergy House at Alfriston, more substantial manor houses like Barrington Court, or castles like Bodiam and Tattershall, these could be considered works of 'natural beauty' almost as much as of 'historic interest'.

It was perhaps only the advance of knowledge about seventeenth- and eighteenth-century architecture, promoted by writers like Sacheverell Sitwell and Christopher Hussey, and by the newly founded Georgian Group, that finally aroused an interest in houses and their contents as a single entity. The appalling loss of pictures, sculpture and furniture through the auction rooms, threatening the existence of these 'corporate works of art', came to be recognised, and, somewhat reluctantly at first, the Trust began to realise it must act, if this great national asset was not to be wholly squandered.

Even with the advent of the Country Houses Scheme, purely architectural standards tended to predominate, however. It was no accident that early houses continued to be most appreciated, from Knole, Blickling and Hardwick to more modest squires' houses like Lytes Cary and Great Chalfield. Petworth was accepted for its internationally famous art collections, but many others – like Montacute, Clandon, Beningbrough and Shugborough – were taken after the dispersal of contents, and the idea of introducing pictures and furniture from other sources to give a lived-in look was still considered perfectly acceptable.

9

Of course, the Trust could only take what houses it was offered, and only when there was a sufficient endowment to maintain them, so its area of choice was always limited. But despite this, the acquisitions of the 1960s and 70s, including Standen, Knightshayes, Cragside and Castle Drogo, showed an increasing respect for Victorian and Edwardian architecture. At the same time there was a greater awareness of the many different aspects of a country house estate: its archaeological remains (like the medieval old hall at Tatton, and the priory buildings at Mottisfont), its industrial monuments (like the wharf at Cotehele, or the mill at Dunham Massey), its domestic offices (most notable at Erddig and Lanhydrock), its home farm (like those at Wimpole and Shugborough).

Nevertheless, a particular worry at this period was the widening gap between the endowment which the Trust needed, and the capital sum which a donor could be expected to raise. It was not until the founding of the National Heritage Memorial Fund in 1979 that another source of funding became available, and the Trust's role in saving houses could become more positive. Significantly, Canons Ashby, the first to be acquired with the Fund's help, and A La Ronde, the most recent, had both been accepted on merit in the earliest days of the Country Houses Scheme, but had consistently fallen down on financial grounds. Nor would Calke and Kedleston have been remotely possible without the assistance of the NHMF: the former of particular importance as a document of social history rather than for its architecture or the quality of its collections.

In recent years, private trusts set up by owners of historic houses have enjoyed almost as much tax relief as the National Trust, and acceptable alternative uses have been found for many houses which remain well protected by the listing system. That has left the Trust more as an ultimate safety net than as a place of first resort for owners in difficulty. Indeed, the adaptation of Cliveden as a luxury hotel has shown that, in the right circumstances, its houses too can profit from an alliance with private enterprise.

Apart from the gradual furnishing of houses which came virtually empty in the early days of the Country Houses Scheme, the Trust has also found partners who could enliven them in other ways. The National Portrait Gallery's displays of Elizabethan and Jacobean, Civil War, and baroque portraits, at Montacute, Gawthorpe and Beningbrough respectively, could hardly represent a more appropriate use, and the same could be said of exhibitions of costume at Killerton, musical instruments at Hatchlands, and the history of photography at Lacock.

On the whole, the Trust has always been conservative in its attitude to the display of historic interiors, preferring to keep the layer-on-layer of different generations, than to return to one particular period. At Ham and Osterley, where these later contributions had been largely removed, it was prepared to support the more purist approach of the Victoria and Albert Museum, which owned the remaining contents and which, from 1949 to 1990, administered both properties on the Trust's behalf.

The few full-scale redecoration schemes the Trust has undertaken itself were an attempt to revive empty or underfurnished houses in the late 1960s and early 70s, with bolder colour schemes and upholstery by John Fowler at Shugborough, Clandon and Sudbury, and by David Mlinaric at Beningbrough. These did not pretend to be archaeologically precise, but were free interpretations based on the paint 'scrapes' then available, and on knowledge of other houses of the same period. But in general the Trust has tried to avoid controversial reconstructions and to let the houses speak for themselves, through the different generations of previous owners, whose portraits gaze down from panelled or damask-covered walls.

Wherever possible, too, the Trust has encouraged these families to retain their links with the properties they gave. It adds immeasurably to visitors' experience of a house to find it still inhabited as a family home, with all the small impedimenta of everyday life – flowers, books, photographs and contemporary works of art – rather than presented as a dead museum.

That also explains the Trust's attitude to 'interpretation': the fashion for spoon-feeding visitors with information, rather than allowing them to discover the history of a place for themselves. As a general policy, free flow has always been preferred to guided tours, and exhibitions, which tend to overshadow or even replace the actual experience of a house, have been kept to a minimum. Stables are obviously more satisfactory full of horses than converted into exhibitions about hunting or racing, and the same applies to brewhouses, bakeries, laundries and all the other buildings supporting a great house. A very important part of this approach has been the provision of informative guidebooks and general literature about the Trust's possessions, making the latest historical research freely available: a service to which it is hoped this book will itself contribute.

The real revolution has not therefore come in the way the Trust's houses are displayed or presented but in the way they are conserved. For a long time, the national museums were pre-eminent in this field, with the Trust seeking their advice and practical help with particular problems. Over the last twenty years, however, a formidable team of conservators has been built up within the organisation. Many eighteenth- and nineteenth-century methods of good housekeeping have been revived, blinds (and ultra-violet filters) have cut down the damaging effects of daylight, case covers have protected precious original upholstery, tapestries have been painstakingly repaired, and the effects of wear and tear carefully monitored. The Trust is also proud to have contributed to the revival of many traditional crafts and materials, from hand-loom weaving and block-printing down to the production of lead paint and limewash.

In its original charter, the National Trust was charged to hold its possessions 'in perpetuity'. The course of natural decay may make that something of a pious hope, but we are now better equipped to make the attempt than at any previous time in our history. Even after the tragedy of the Uppark fire, we can look forward with optimism to its rebirth, confident that its haunting beauty will be recaptured.

This book, devoted to the Trust's country houses, is not just a catalogue recalling past achievements, but a celebration of a living tradition that has never enjoyed greater popularity or greater support.

Gervase Jackson-Stops
Architectural Adviser to the National Trust

Chapter One

Changing Hands

THE NATIONAL TRUST AND COUNTRY HOUSES

Alas! how curious it is that these works of art only begin to obtain a wide appreciation when they are on the verge of being destroyed. What country houses of any size, one wonders, can hope to survive the next fifty years?

Osbert Sitwell, 1935

In 1928 the architect Clough Williams-Ellis announced the death of the country house. 'It is a fact, patent to all and deplored by some, that the large-scale private paradise is already obsolescent.' The obituary notice, which appeared in his *England and the Octopus*, an angry piece of conservationist polemic, gave a number of reasons for the country house's demise: changes in the social order, which led many owners to 'abdicate from a position that they find uncongenial and slightly ridiculous'; crippling taxation; poor estate management; and 'expensive tastes incompatible with the low returns from landowning'.

But if the country house as an institution was dead, Williams-Ellis wasn't about to let it lie down. It was inconceivable that this unique synthesis of architecture, contents, setting and historical associations should be allowed to disappear simply because shifts in the structure of post-war society were eroding the power of the class that had created it. Yet the inconceivable was happening, and something must be done to stop it, not because of any sense of loyalty to that class, but because the country house belonged, in a sense, to everybody. It was part of our common inheritance, part of what the 1920s called 'the national treasure'.

Williams-Ellis's solution was simple. A commission should be set up to list those

Philip Kerr, 11th Marquess of Lothian: 'If a body like the National Trust were willing to equip itself to become a landlord on an ampler scale, it would gradually draw within its orbit quite a large number of historic furnished houses.' (*The National Trust*)

13

country houses which really deserved protection 'as national monuments and as characteristic and precious parts of England'. The buildings on that list would be scheduled, and their owners would be exempted from rates and certain taxes; in return, they would open their doors to the public, under carefully framed conditions, and agree to refer any alterations to a statutory body set up for the purpose.

In the years that followed, others took up the challenge. In January 1930, a *Country Life* editorial headed 'Our National Inheritance' called on the government to 'do something practical to prevent the constant breaking up of beautiful properties into ugly building estates and the dispersal abroad of well-nigh priceless collections':

> The state has already exempted from death duties works of art of public interest. Why should it not extend this principle to parks and woods and open spaces such as those of Goodwood, which, though privately owned, are always open for public enjoyment, and to houses such as Knole, which are in reality national treasure houses of beautiful things?

That the country house was in crisis, that the 'breaking up of beautiful properties' was reaching epidemic proportions, was not in doubt. Throughout the twenties, great estate after great estate was falling prey to developers and speculators. Income tax, land tax and rates were taking more than 30 per cent of estate rentals; in 1919 death duties, first introduced in 1894, were increased to 40 per cent on estates worth more than £2 million; and during the slump in land values that followed the end of the war some six million acres had come under new ownership. 'England is changing hands,' lamented *The Times* in May 1920, as collections which had taken centuries to assemble were dispersed at auction. Staircases, chimneypieces, ceilings, whole rooms were stripped out and sold off;[1] and hundreds of country houses were pulled down, their walls reduced to rubble. But individual calls for the government to do something to alleviate the crisis had about as much effect as individual calls on the government usually have. What was needed was some organisation to coordinate the campaign, to act as an umbrella under which the disparate band of conservative noblemen and crusading radicals could gather.

In many ways, the National Trust was a natural candidate for the job. Formed in 1895 as a private charity dedicated to acquiring and protecting 'Places of Historic Interest or Natural Beauty', it was already just such an unlikely alliance of landowners and radicals. Moreover, it had practical experience of the problems involved in maintaining country houses. The buildings in its care included the sixteenth-century Barrington Court in Somerset, which had been bought in 1907, largely with the help of a £10,000 donation from a Miss J. L. Woodward, and which

---

1 And sometimes whole houses. A rather mysterious entrepreneur named George Ferdinando bought Basildon Park in Berkshire in the 1920s and offered to dismantle it and re-erect it anywhere in America for one million dollars. There were no takers, although some of the plasterwork found its way to the Waldorf Astoria in New York, which still boasts a Basildon Room.

Barrington Court, Somerset: the National Trust's first country house, acquired in 1907.
(*NTPL/Neil Campbell-Sharp*)

had nevertheless proved to be an enormous burden until 1920, when in return for a long lease Colonel A. A. Lyle agreed to restore it. The Trust's other major country house, the late-Elizabethan Montacute, also in Somerset, which had failed to find a buyer when it came on to the market in 1929 and two years later was being offered at a scrap-value of £5,882, had been bought by the Society for the Protection of Ancient Buildings in 1931. It was handed over to the Trust in the following year – an act of generosity made possible only by a further act of generosity, a cheque for £30,000 for its purchase and upkeep, given by the philanthropist Ernest Cook.

At a National Trust dinner in 1933 the Director of the Courtauld Institute, Professor W. G. Constable, said that the organisation must act, and act quickly, to preserve the country house – by which he meant that it should launch in earnest the campaign that Clough Williams-Ellis, *Country Life* and others had called for. And then in July 1934, Philip Kerr, 11th Marquess of Lothian, gave a speech at the

Trust's annual meeting at Inner Temple Hall. He asked whether the Trust might not extend its protection – which, in spite of Barrington and Montacute, had until then been largely confined to areas of coast and countryside, and smaller vernacular buildings – to 'another part of our national treasure . . . the historic dwelling houses of this country'.

In fact the main target of Lothian's speech was not the Trust, but the Treasury. He had been hard-hit by death duties on succeeding in 1930 to his cousin's title and estates, which included Blickling in Norfolk, and the experience had left scars. When Lloyd George wrote to congratulate him on his inheritance, he had replied: 'I shall have to pay to our exhausted Exchequer almost forty per cent of the capital value of a mainly agricultural estate. In my capacity as an ordinary citizen I think highly of these arrangements but as an inheritor of a title and estates thereto they will prove somewhat embarrassing.' In his speech to the Trust four years later, he said that most country houses were under sentence of death, 'and the axe which was destroying them was taxation, and especially that form of taxation known as death duties'. (The audience cheered.) The Trust should draw up a list of mansions of national importance, and lobby the government to make certain concessions. Scheduled houses should be exempt from death duties unless they were sold, or even if they were sold, provided that they were preserved as a whole; their owners should be allowed to set against tax any money spent on upkeep or restoration; and if these measures failed, a property should be de-rated.

Like most campaigners of the time, Lothian's chief concern was to find a way whereby an owner could continue to live in his ancestral home. Hence his emphasis on changes in fiscal policy. 'Nothing is more melancholy than to visit these ancient houses after they have been turned into public museums,' he said. 'If they are to be preserved, they must be maintained, save for a few great palaces, for the uses for which they were designed.' But he closed his speech with one last suggestion, one that was eventually to have tremendous implications for both the National Trust and the country house – so tremendous that his words, reported in *The Times*, deserve to be quoted at length:

> Why should not the National Trust equip itself to hold properties bequeathed, or given to it, or acquired by it, on terms not unlike those which governed Lord Lee's munificent gift of Chequers? He believed that if a body like the National Trust were willing to equip itself to become a landlord on an ampler scale, it would gradually draw within its orbit quite a large number of historic furnished houses. The essence of the case was that the houses should be both furnished and sufficiently modernised in their domestic arrangements to be easily let, and, if possible, should have enough land or endowment to cover the cost of maintaining the structure. The Trust could then seek suitable tenants, using the rents it received either for improvements or to balance expenses on houses it could not let.

As things stood in 1934, Lothian's suggestion that the charity should itself 'become a landlord on an ampler scale' must have seemed far too daunting a prospect, especially in view of the Trust's experience in trying to maintain Barrington Court.

In any case, an Act of Parliament would have been necessary to enable the Trust to take on a house, its contents and estate, together with an endowment in the form of land or investments to pay for maintenance.

But Lothian's speech did mark the beginning of a concerted campaign to save the country house. It was followed three months later by another speech, this time by W. Harding Thompson, who told the national conference of the Council for the Preservation of Rural England that a survey should immediately be carried out to establish which houses were worth saving, and that an owners' association should be set up to lobby the Treasury for the 'remission of duties in approved cases in exchange for regulated public access at specified times'. This was the line which the National Trust itself took. In February 1936 its Secretary, Macleod Matheson, arranged a reception to launch a new federation of owners. Its aims, said the Trust's chairman, Lord Zetland, would be to compile a list of the most important houses, which would be approved by the Office of Works; to offer access and information to the public; and – last, but certainly not least – to 'endeavour to obtain, in the interest of the preservation of a national heritage of great historical and artistic value, some relief from the burden of taxation'.

The idea met with a deafening silence. Country house owners, reluctant to give up their independence, gave it little encouragement. And the government was understandably rather wary about the political consequences of awarding tax concessions to a group that was still perceived by the majority of voters to be the wealthiest class in society, even if such concessions were to be given in return for guaranteed public access.

Faced with such a stalemate, the Trust launched its own initiative. Lord Zetland and Macleod Matheson decided that if Parliament could be persuaded to pass the legislation necessary to overcome a daunting array of obstacles, such as the difficulty of breaking entails, and the likely infringement of the laws of property involved in an owner's giving a house and estate to a charity and then continuing to live in it, the Trust would indeed become a 'landlord on an ampler scale'. It would accept country houses and their contents and estates, with the proviso that an endowment in the form of land or money should also be given to enable the property to be maintained. The newly appointed secretary of the Trust's Historic Country Houses Committee, James Lees-Milne, drew up the list of important houses that everyone had been demanding for so long; and the owners of those houses – some 250 in all – were canvassed for their opinions. The attractions of the scheme, both to the owner of a country house and to the general public, were outlined in a *Times* leader in October 1936:

> The advantage to the owner combines freedom from responsibility with the assurance that the connection of his family with the family seat shall not be sharply and completely broken. The advantage to the public combines freedom of access to treasures of natural and artistic beauty with the preservation of the character and occupation which makes the difference between a dwelling and a museum, a country place and a public playground.

Parliament did pass the required new legislation, in the form of the two National

Trust Acts of 1937 and 1939; the Country Houses Scheme, as it was called, was launched; and the National Trust, by default rather than by design, embarked on a path which would turn it into the largest holder of country houses in Britain.

There is a certain irony in the fact that the first country house to come to the National Trust in the late 1930s was no venerable mansion of antiquity, but a building only eight years older than the Trust itself. In 1936 Sir Geoffrey Mander, the owner of the late-Victorian Wightwick Manor near Wolverhampton in the West Midlands, heard from his friend Sir Charles Trevelyan that he was negotiating to leave his eighteenth-century home at Wallington in Northumberland to the Trust. (In fact Trevelyan made it over during his lifetime, stating in a press release in November 1941 that he 'had a double motive for his action. He is a Socialist and believes it would be better if the community owned such houses and great estates. He was also influenced by Lord Lothian with whom he discussed the whole question some years ago.') Trevelyan's idea appealed to Mander. Fortunately – and quite remarkably, considering the low regard for all things Victorian between the wars – it appealed to the National Trust as well, and in 1937 Wightwick became the first of the new wave of Trust acquisitions.

However, in the beginning that wave seemed more like a ripple. By the end of 1941 the Trust had acquired Wightwick, Wallington and Blickling (left by Lord Lothian, who had died in December 1940). Hatchlands in Surrey had been offered by the architectural historian H. S. Goodhart-Rendel, and accepted; Stourhead in Wiltshire had been promised; and Old Devonshire House in Bloomsbury, London, had been given and then destroyed by German bombs. Seven other negotiations had foundered for one reason or another, including Canons Ashby in Northampton-shire, where the owner had died and his successor held different ideas about the future of the house.

In February 1942 Lord Esher, chairman of the Trust's Country Houses Committee, was expressing concern about the slow progress of the scheme: 'I am disturbed by the failure of the Trust to obtain any considerable number of country houses, and by the apparent difficulty of reaching agreement between the Trust and those owners who have shown an inclination to take advantage of our services.' A major sticking point was the question of an endowment. Then, as now, the Trust required enough land or capital to maintain the house, and many owners were understandably rather cautious about the idea of making over most or all of their ancestral estates to a small private charity.

But still houses did continue to come, thanks largely to the untiring efforts of James Lees-Milne, who resumed his duties as secretary to the Country Houses Committee after being invalided out of the army in 1940, and spent the rest of the war travelling the country, negotiating with prospective donors. By 1945, the National Trust's fiftieth anniversary, the charity held seventeen country houses, ranging from the black-and-white splendours of Little Moreton Hall in Cheshire and Speke Hall, Merseyside, to West Wycombe Park in Buckinghamshire, with Nicholas Revett's Greek Revival portico, and the Victorian Italianate of Charles Barry's Cliveden, also in Buckinghamshire.

In the same year, the election of Attlee's Labour government sent a frisson of fear through the country house-owning classes. A series of *Country Life* articles on 'The Future of Great Country Houses' which appeared in the November, four months after the general election, was defensive, almost paranoid, in its efforts to justify private ownership – as if the writers, all owners of country houses, were afraid that Attlee and his Chancellor of the Exchequer, Hugh Dalton, were set to storm the Winter Palace. Privilege means public service, declared Burghley's Marchioness of Exeter, and all the privileged ask 'is that they may be permitted to continue to serve and that the scales shall not be too unfairly weighted against them.' Meanwhile Christopher Hussey, architectural editor of *Country Life* and donor (in 1970) of Scotney Castle and Garden in Kent, was anxious 'for the electorate to disabuse itself of the common confusion between a great historic house and housing': 'It has not been seriously suggested that these buildings could materially contribute to the housing shortage, hopelessly situated and designed as they are to that purpose, yet the feeling is probably at the back of the minds of some people who regard the great house as somehow inimical to their just aspirations.'

But in the context of the country house at least, the most revolutionary measure enacted by Attlee and Dalton was to set aside £50 million for the creation of a National Land Fund, which was to be used to acquire property for preservation as a memorial to those who had died in the war. Such property would be passed on to an approved organisation. Dalton also revived a little-used provision in the 1910 Finance Act which had allowed property to be given to the Inland Revenue in lieu of tax, and proposed that in future 'much more use should be made of this power to accept land in payment of death duties'.

There were some who saw these measures as the first steps towards the compulsory nationalisation of historic houses. But their immediate effect was to make it much easier for owners to leave their houses to the National Trust, which was one of the organisations recognised by the Treasury as a suitable recipient for property given in lieu of estate duty. In 1947, on the death of the 5th Earl of Mount Edgcumbe, Cotehele House in Cornwall – described by James Lees-Milne at the time as a West Country Knole – was the first country house to be transferred to the Trust through National Land Fund procedures. Far from storming the Winter Palace, the Attlee administration had done more than any previous government to ensure that the country house would be preserved for all time, and that, if they chose to do so, those who lived in it might continue to enjoy their occupancy.

As the number of country houses held by the National Trust continued to grow, and as the public demand to see and enjoy them grew with it, it became apparent that the pre-war ideal – that once transferred to the Trust, a house should simply continue as it always had, without any change save that of legal ownership – would have to be modified. The more extravagant private schemes to turn 'stately homes' into profitable tourist enterprises, complete with safari parks and other attractions, were scorned by the Trust. (In 1966 Lord Antrim, then chairman, announced to the annual general meeting that the organisation's job was 'not to involve itself in the entertainment industry. We take over these places to keep them in their natural state, and not to provide more holiday camps.') But it was clear that the Trust must adopt a more positive role in presenting its historic houses to the visitor; clear, too,

that public access – which when the Country Houses Scheme was first mooted in the 1930s had been seen as of secondary importance – was coming to be a vital factor, something which, while never eclipsing the Trust's primary duty to conserve for posterity a building, its contents and its setting, could no longer be left to chance.

The situation was complicated (as indeed it still is) by the different circumstances in which country houses came to the Trust. Some, like Uppark in West Sussex (acquired in 1954), Dyrham in Avon (1961) and Felbrigg in Norfolk (1969), were intact, fully furnished, and quite perfect as they were. For these, change was unthinkable – the Trust's job was simply to preserve them. Others were already in decline, or for one reason or another were empty of all furniture; and on these houses the Trust was forced to impose its own taste in furnishings and interior decoration. Clandon Park, Surrey (1956); Beningbrough Hall, Yorkshire (1958); and Sudbury Hall, Derbyshire (1967), all fall into that category. At Sudbury, for example, a house with state rooms that were sparsely furnished, but that contained the most exquisite Caroline plasterwork and carvings, John Fowler – who acted as the Trust's adviser on interior decoration during the 1960s and 1970s – chose not to fill those rooms with furniture and textiles that had no connection with the house, but instead to emphasise the existing decorative features. In a move that aroused considerable controversy at the time, the balustrade of the staircase, which was covered in layers of graining and varnish, was stripped and painted white; the plaster ceiling above it was painted in two tones to throw its decoration into high relief; and the walls were given a coat of strong yellow ochre. The overall effect may not have any precedent in the Caroline period – but it works, and Fowler's interiors have themselves become part of Sudbury's history.

All the same, ideas have changed and scholarship has advanced in the decades since the redecoration of Sudbury Hall. Today the National Trust cares for some two hundred historic houses and castles in England, Wales and Northern Ireland, from the fourteenth-century Bodiam (Sussex), that most romantic of all medieval ruins, to Castle Drogo (Devon), the Lutyens fantasy equipped with all modern conveniences, which was only completed in 1930 – two years after Clough Williams-Ellis announced the death of the country house. And in the fifty years or more which have passed since the inception of the Country Houses Scheme, the Trust's response to the conservation and interpretation of those buildings – and in many cases, their surrounding estates – has inevitably changed to take account of an ever more complex range of issues and expectations.

When, for example, Erddig in Clwyd was acquired in 1973, the unusually rich evidence of life below stairs led to a departure from the traditional practice of bringing visitors into the house through the front door. Instead, they are steered through the estate yard, with its smithy, joiner's shop and bakery, and in through the servants' entrance. The social structures at Erddig are every bit as interesting as the art-objects and the interiors, and the presentation of the house reflects this. And

Clandon Park, Surrey: the morning room, redecorated in the 1960s by John Fowler.
(*NTPL/Erik Pelham*)

Calke Abbey, Derbyshire: even a time-capsule needs a sound roof. Fundamental conservation work was necessary following the National Trust's acquisition of the house in 1985. (*NTPL/Rob Matheson*)

at Calke Abbey in Derbyshire, taken over in 1985, the decision was made to preserve the peculiar 'time-capsule' quality of the house – where virtually nothing has been thrown away since the mid-nineteenth century – by deliberately limiting the extent of the restoration. Paintings were left with their layers of darkened varnish. Dilapidated furniture was made sound, but was not over-polished. Interiors were repaired as necessary, but (with a couple of exceptions) were not redecorated.

A completely different approach has been adopted at Uppark in West Sussex, which was devastated by fire in August 1989. Here the Trust was faced with some difficult choices. Should it complete the fire's work and demolish what remained; or make the ruins safe and leave them as a memorial to a once-great house? Or should it embark on a major rebuilding programme to restore Uppark to its former glory? It chose this last course, a decision which reflects Uppark's enormous architectural importance, but which has left the organisation facing perhaps the greatest challenge in its long history.

The National Trust's policy towards each building is to respond to its uniqueness, to provide different solutions for different problems of restoration, interpretation and presentation. The problems change with the years. And so must the solutions, since the fact that a country house changes hands, the fact that its ownership shifts from the individual to the collective, need not, and must not, mean that it loses those qualities that made us all value it in the first place.

But what *are* those qualities? As we walk through the great halls and long galleries, we think – a little guiltily, perhaps – about what fun it must have been to live in them (always the master or mistress, never the servant). Depending on our political stance, we wallow in nostalgia for a vanished age, or rejoice in the downfall of the class that built them. But only the most hardened philistine can fail to be moved by their most potent appeal – their sheer beauty, the creative vision of the artists and craftsmen who made them.

And in the end, the Trust's historic houses must speak for themselves: it is the personal experience of that beauty, that creative vision, which justifies all the time

Uppark, Sussex: its restoration after a major fire in 1989 is one of the greatest challenges the National Trust has ever faced. In the first phase of restoration the whole house was enclosed in a weatherproof skin. (*NTPL/Will Webster*)

and money involved in their preservation. Of the thirty houses described in detail in the following pages, some would probably have survived intact if the Trust had not existed; some would perhaps have adapted to changing circumstances, becoming schools, or hotels, or business centres. But others might have disappeared – and their loss would have impoverished us all. It would be facile to suggest that the National Trust has single-handedly saved the country house from extinction – government grants, tax concessions, rising land values and a buoyant market for works of art have all played their part. But there is no doubt that because, nearly sixty years ago, a small private charity, with few members and even fewer resources, was forced to put itself forward as a guardian of our architectural heritage, reports of the death of the country house have been greatly exaggerated.